Portugal

by Ariel Factor Birdoff

Consultant: Marjorie Faulstich Orellana, PhD
Professor of Urban Schooling
University of California, Los Angeles

BEARPORT
PUBLISHING

New York, New York

Credits

Cover, © viki2win/iStock and © Nataliya Nazarova/Shutterstock; TOC, © mkos83/iStock; 4, © Charles03/iStock; 5T, © Zhukova Valentyna/Shutterstock; 5B, © Tropical studio/Shutterstock; 7, © RossHelen/iStock; 8, © dabldy/iStock; 9T, © bennymarty/iStock; 9B, © Ruigouveia/Dreamstime; 10T, © CSP_josemoura/Fotosearch LBRF/AGE Fotostock; 10B, © John Cuyos/Shutterstock; 11T, © Duncan Usher/Ardea/AGE Fotostock; 11B, © Marco Govel/Shutterstock; 12T, © Michael Reusse/AGE Fotostock; 12B, © Mario Rodrigues/Shutterstock; 13, © Mauricio Abreu/Alamy; 13B, © Lisa S./Shutterstock; 14, © StockPhotosArt/iStock; 15T, © krivinis/Shutterstock; 15B, © saiko3p/Shutterstock; 16T, © Inge Hogenbijl/Dreamstime; 16B, © Sylvain Grandadam/AGE Fotostock; 17, © jackmalipan/iStock; 18, © Michal Stipek/iStock; 18–19, © SeanPavonePhoto/iStock; 20, © Michael Stipek/iStock; 21, © Mangostar/Shutterstock; 22, © JackF/iStock; 23, © hiphoto/Shutterstock; 24, © Maridav/Shutterstock; 25, © kivni/Shutterstock; 26L, © Dmytro Larin/Shutterstock; 26–27, © Luciano_Quieroz/iStock; 28–29, © urf/iStock; 30T, © Viktor Kunz/Shutterstock and © spinetta/Shutterstock; 30B, © DimaBerkut/iStock; 31 (T to B), © Nicolas Lum/Alamy, © moedas1/iStock, © Syda Productions/Shutterstock, © Stefan Malloch/Shutterstock, © Christian Balate/Shutterstock, © dabldy/iStock, and © chrisdorney/Shutterstock; 32, © Boris15/Shutterstock.

Publisher: Kenn Goin
Senior Editor: Joyce Tavolacci
Creative Director: Spencer Brinker
Design: Debrah Kaiser
Photo Researcher: Thomas Persano

Library of Congress Cataloging-in-Publication Data

Names: Birdoff, Ariel Factor, author.
Title: Portugal / by Ariel Factor Birdoff.
Description: New York, New York : Bearport Publishing, [2019] | Series:
   Countries we come from | Includes bibliographical references and index.
Identifiers: LCCN 2018044158 (print) | LCCN 2018044965 (ebook) | ISBN
   9781642802634 (ebook) | ISBN 9781642801941 (library bound)
Subjects: LCSH: Portugal—Juvenile literature.
Classification: LCC DP517 (ebook) | LCC DP517 .B47 2019 (print) | DDC
   946.9—dc23
LC record available at https://lccn.loc.gov/2018044158

For more information, write to Bearport Publishing Company, Inc., 45 West 21st Street, Suite 3B, New York, New York 10010. Printed in the United States of America.

10 9 8 7 6 5 4 3 2 1

Contents

Stunning

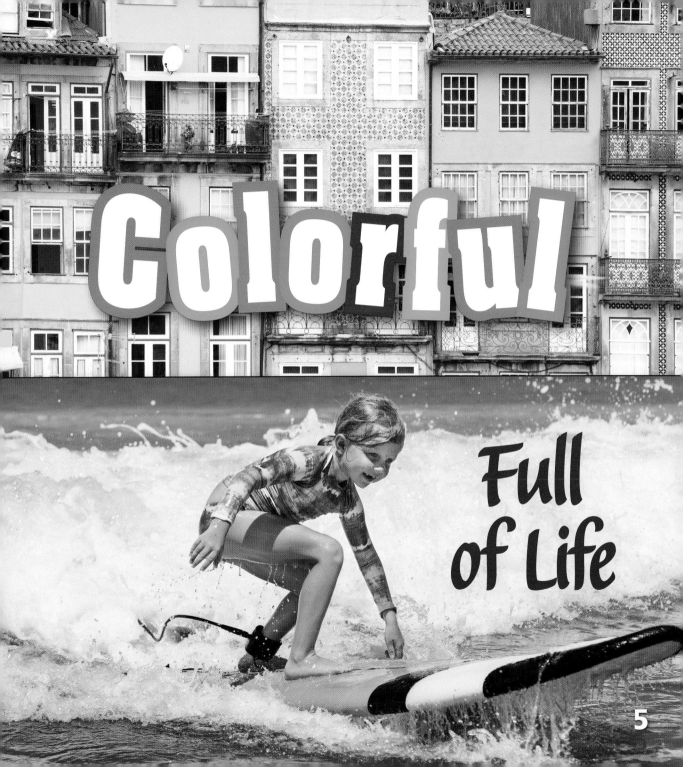

Colorful

Full of Life

Welcome to Portugal!
Portugal is a country in Europe.
It's located on the Iberian **Peninsula**.

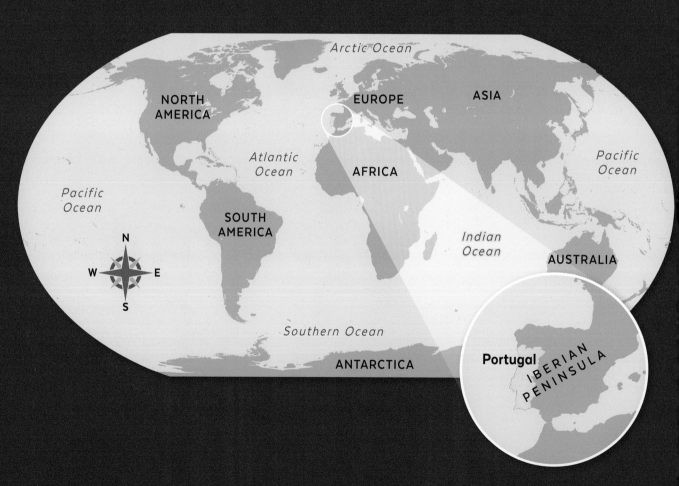

Over 10 million people live in Portugal.

Portugal has a long coast with beautiful beaches.

The beaches attract many visitors.

People come to sunbathe.

Portugal is known for big waves and surfing.

The coast is rich in wildlife.

Crabs and clams live in the water close to shore.

Sardines and tuna swim in deeper waters.

hares

Portugal is home to
many land animals, too.
There are boars, hares,
and **rare** Iberian lynxes!

For work, some people fish in the rich ocean waters.

Others collect **minerals**, such as salt.

workers shoveling salt

Some Portuguese work as farmers.

They often grow grapes, olives, and tomatoes.

cork

Most of the world's cork is grown in Portugal. Cork is a special kind of tree bark. It's used to plug wine bottles!

13

Portugal has a long history.
It was settled over 2,000 years ago.

In ancient Portugal,
people built *dolmens*.
A dolmen is a stone
building used as a tomb.

Over many years, different groups ruled the land.

Moorish castle

Roman temple

These people included the Romans, Moors, and Iberians.

15

In the 700s, the Moors started making tiles in Portugal.

Today, the country is famous for its handpainted tiles and pottery!

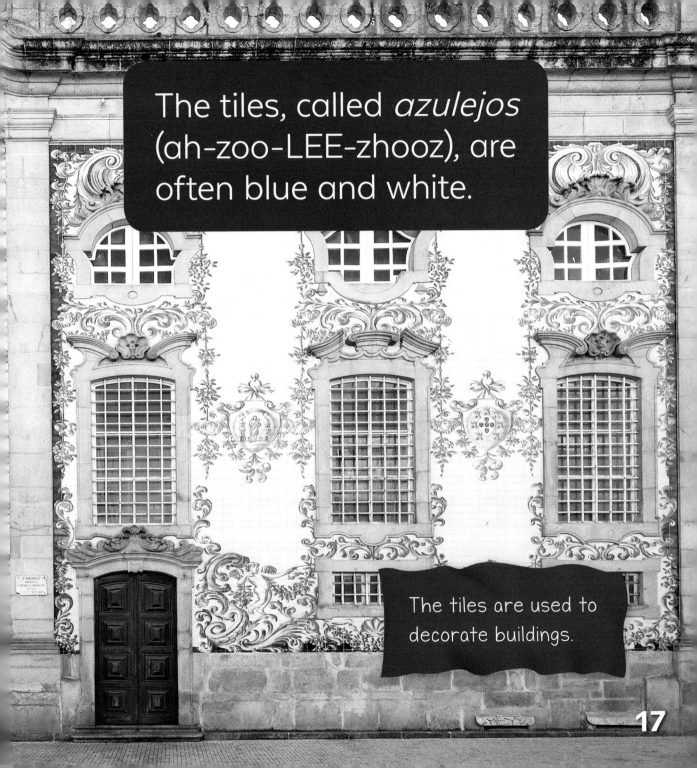

The tiles, called *azulejos* (ah-zoo-LEE-zhooz), are often blue and white.

The tiles are used to decorate buildings.

The **capital** of Portugal is Lisbon.

It's also the country's largest city.

More than 1.5 million people live there.

Oporto is the second-largest city in Portugal.

Lisbon

Portuguese is the main language in Portugal.

This is how you say *good morning* in Portuguese:

Bom dia (BOM DEE-ah)

This is how you say *thank you*:

Obrigado (oh-bree-GAH-doh)

or

Obrigada (oh-bree-GAH-dah)

Worldwide, over 200 million people speak Portuguese.

Portuguese food is fresh and hearty.

It often includes meat, fish, rice, and beans.

Stews and soups are very popular.

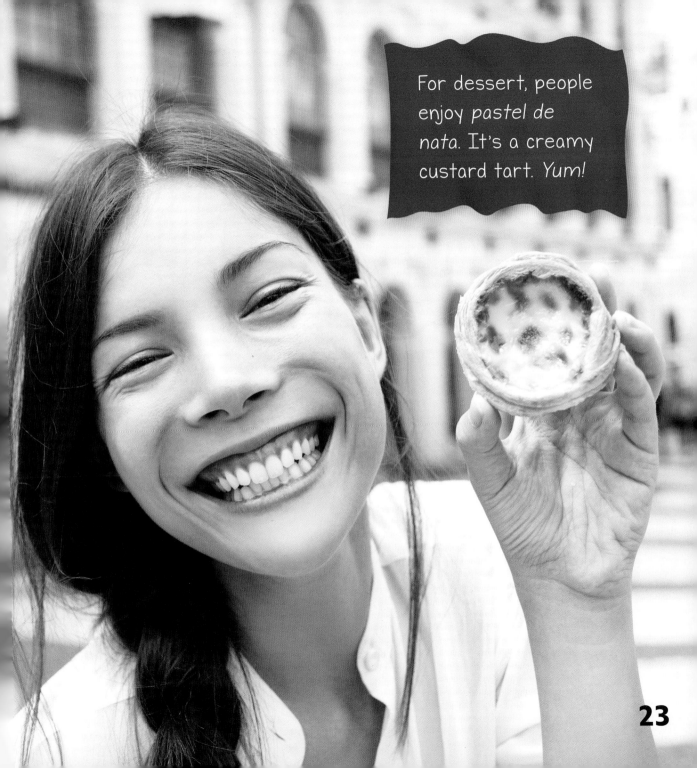

For dessert, people enjoy *pastel de nata*. It's a creamy custard tart. Yum!

23

What's the most popular sport in Portugal?

People love soccer! The country has over 35 teams.

Futsal (FOOT-sal) is another popular sport. It's like soccer but played indoors.

Let's sing and dance!

Portugal is known for its folk music.

It's played with guitars and mandolins.

mandolin

People enjoy dancing to the lively music.

Fado (FAH-doo) is a type of Portuguese song. It's often about something sad.

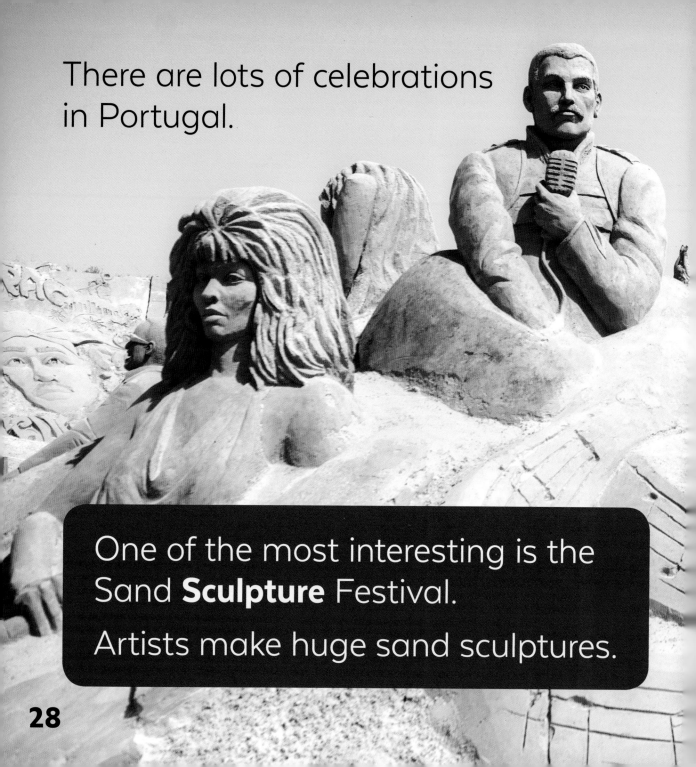

There are lots of celebrations in Portugal.

One of the most interesting is the Sand **Sculpture** Festival.

Artists make huge sand sculptures.

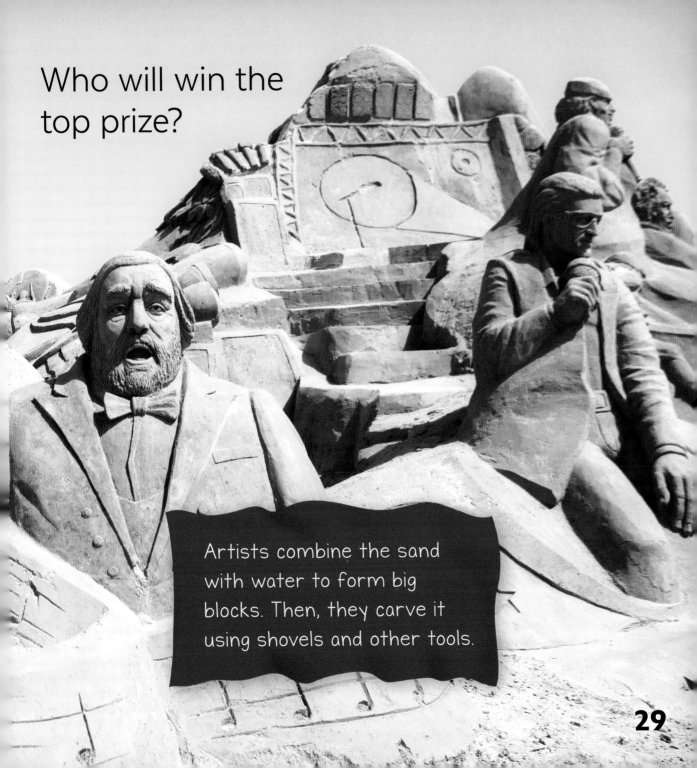

Who will win the top prize?

Artists combine the sand with water to form big blocks. Then, they carve it using shovels and other tools.

Fast Facts

Capital city: Lisbon

Population of Portugal:
About 10 million

Main language:
Portuguese

Money: Euro

Major religion:
Roman Catholic

Neighboring country:
Spain

Cool Fact: Lisbon is home to the world's oldest bookstore. It dates from 1732!

capital (KAP-uh-tuhl) the city where a country's government is based

minerals (MIN-ur-uhlz) solid substances, such as quartz, found in nature

peninsula (puh-NIN-soo-lah) land surrounded by water on three sides

rare (RAIR) not often seen or found

sculpture (SKULP-chur) a statue or object made by carving or molding

31

Index

Read More

Deckker, Zilah. *Portugal (Countries of the World).* Washington, DC: National Geographic (2009).

Schuetz, Kari. *Portugal (Exploring Countries).* Minnetonka, MN: Bellwether (2012).

Learn More Online

To learn more about Portugal, visit
www.bearportpublishing.com/CountriesWeComeFrom

About the Author

Ariel Factor Birdoff lives in New York City with her husband. She once traveled to Portugal and hopes to return to the Iberian Peninsula one day soon.